# 60 Great HORROR Movie Posters

volume nineteen of
the illustrated history of movies through posters

Images from the Hershenson-Allen Archive

Published by Bruce Hershenson
P.O. Box 874, West Plains, MO 65775
Phone: (417) 256-9616  Fax: (417) 257-6948
mail@brucehershenson.com (e-mail)
http://www.brucehershenson.com or
http://www.emovieposter.com (website)

IF YOU ENJOYED THIS MOVIE POSTER BOOK, THEN YOU ARE SURE

TO ENJOY THESE OTHER SIMILAR BRUCE HERSHENSON

PUBLICATIONS. LOOK FOR THEM AT YOUR LOCAL BOOKSTORE OR

ORDER THEM DIRECT FROM THE PUBLISHER.

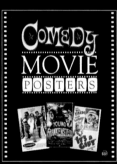
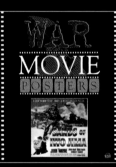

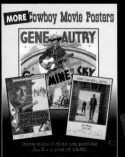

# INTRODUCTION

Welcome to a new series of full-color movie poster books from Bruce Hershenson Publishing! Over the past nine years I have published eighteen volumes of a series of full-color books called the Illustrated History of Movies Through Posters. Each of those volumes is devoted to a specific genre or category of film (horror, cowboy, crime, Academy Award Winners, etc) and each contains hundreds of full-color images from that genre, each containing the finest color printing there is, equal or superior to that found in coffee table books costing several times the price!

While these books have been extremely well received by collectors and movie buffs world-wide, the one request I have regularly received since I began publishing has been to include more full-page images in each volume (in order to give a wide-ranging overview of each topic, I needed to print five images on most pages, although each volume has some full-page images). But I certainly understand a small image does not do justice to these great posters, and I have always agonized when deciding which posters will be given a full page!

That is why I have made this major change to the series. Each new volume in this series now contains sixty of the finest posters from a single genre, with EVERY poster receiving a full-page and each volume is printed with the exact same standards of quality of the earlier series. Since the cover price of each volume is just $14.99, that means the cost per image is just 25 cents!

For this volume, 60 Great Horror Movie Posters (and for the second volume I published at the same time, 60 Great Sci-Fi Movie Posters), I was faced with a difficult question. Exactly where is the dividing line between "horror", "sci-fi" (and "fantasy")? I don,t believe there is a good answer to this question! In my view, horror films must contain a desire to scare the viewers, and should have fantastic elements that could never happen in reality. Sci-fi films should be solidly based in reality, with elements that may well be possible someday, thanks to advances in science. Fantasy films should contain some contrary-to-fact elements (like magic or backward time-travel), but should not be based on a desire to scare the viewer.

But even with these loose definitions, assigning films to these genres is still very difficult, so in the end I just took my best guess and divided these genres into two groups, putting all those films I deemed as "horror" in 60 Great Horror Movie Posters, and all those films I deemed as "sci-fi" or "fantasy" in 60 Great Sci-Fi Movie Posters!

Where did the images in this book come from? They are contained within the archive I co-own with my partner, Richard Allen, the Hershenson-Allen Archive. The archive consists of over 35,000 different movie poster images, all photographed directly from the original posters onto high quality 4" x 5" color transparencies. There is not another resource like it anywhere, and it is the world,s foremost source of movie poster images. The Archive has provided images for books, videos, DVDs, magazines, and newspapers

All of the images in this volume are of the original U.S. one-sheet poster (the standard movie poster size, measuring 27" x 41"), from the first release of the film. There are certainly many other size horror posters (and posters from other countries) that are superlative, and I hope to include those in a future volume of this series.

This is not a catalog of posters for sale, nor do I sell any sort of movie poster reproductions! However, I do sell movie posters of all sorts through auctions, primarily over the Internet, and in the past 14 years I have sold over 17 million dollars of movie paper! If you are interested in acquiring original vintage movie posters (or any of the other 34 books I have published) visit my website at **http://www.brucehershenson.com** (the most visited vintage movie poster site on the Internet with over 500,000 visitors to date) or send a self-addressed stamped envelope to the address on the title page for free brochures.

I need to thank Amy Knight who did the layouts and designed the covers for this book, and Courier Graphics, who printed it. Most of all, I need to thank my partner, Richard Allen. He has always loved movie posters of all years and genres, and he helped track down the images in this book. We share a common vision, and we hope to keep publishing these volumes until we have covered every possible genre of film.

I dedicate this book to my youngest son, Samson Russell Hershenson, who recently celebrated his first birthday. He may be the smallest of my children (only temporarily, I am sure!), but he certainly makes his presence known!

**Bruce Hershenson**
**June 2003**

## GLOSSARY

1

A THRILLING
FANTASTIC
PHOTO-PLAY

# THE CABINET OF
# DR. CALIGARI
## DISTRIBUTED BY GOLDWYN

J.H. TOOKER
PRINT CO.
N.Y.

A UNIVERSAL
PRODUCTION
CARL LAEMMLE
PRESENTS
"THE PHANTOM
OF THE OPERA"
With LON CHANEY
NORMAN KERRY
MARY PHILBIN
AND A CAST OF 5000 OTHERS
STORY BY GASTON LEROUX
DIRECTED BY RUPERT JULIAN
Morgan
"COUNTRY OF ORIGIN, U.S.A."

3

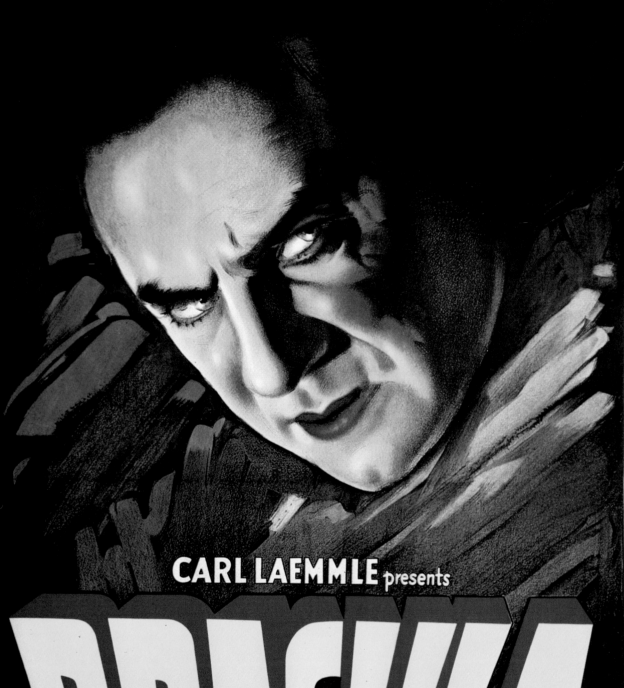

CARL LAEMMLE presents

"DRACULA"

with

BELA LUGOSI
DAVID MANNERS
HELEN CHANDLER
DWIGHT FRYE and
EDWARD VAN SLOAN

A TOD BROWNING Production

FROM THE FAMOUS NOVEL AND PLAY BY BRAM STOKER
PRODUCED BY CARL LAEMMLE Jr.

UNIVERSAL PICTURE

*The story of the strangest Passion the world has ever known!*

WARNING!
THE MONSTER
IS LOOSE!

FRANKENSTEIN

CARL LAEMMLE presents

# FRANKENSTEIN

## THE MAN WHO MADE A MONSTER

with

**COLIN CLIVE, MAE CLARKE, JOHN BOLES, BORIS KARLOFF,** DWIGHT FRYE, EDW. VAN SLOAN & FREDERIC KERR

Based upon the Mary Wollstonecroft Shelley Story

Adapted by John L. Balderston from the play by Peggy Webling

DIRECTED BY JAMES WHALE     A UNIVERSAL PICTURE     PRODUCED BY CARL LAEMMLE, JR.

9

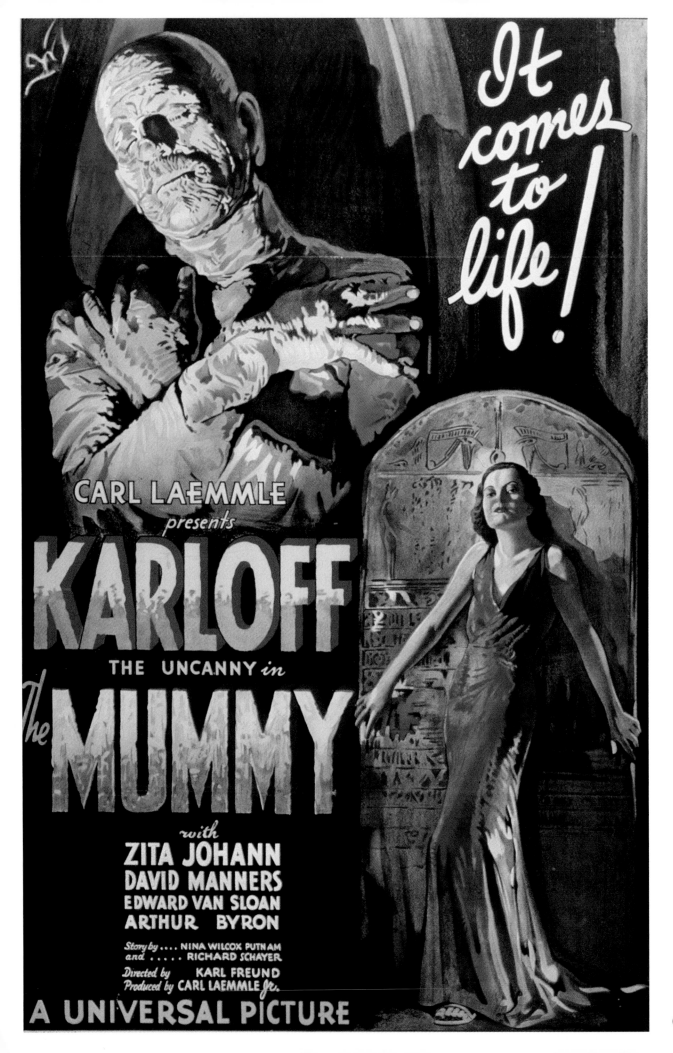

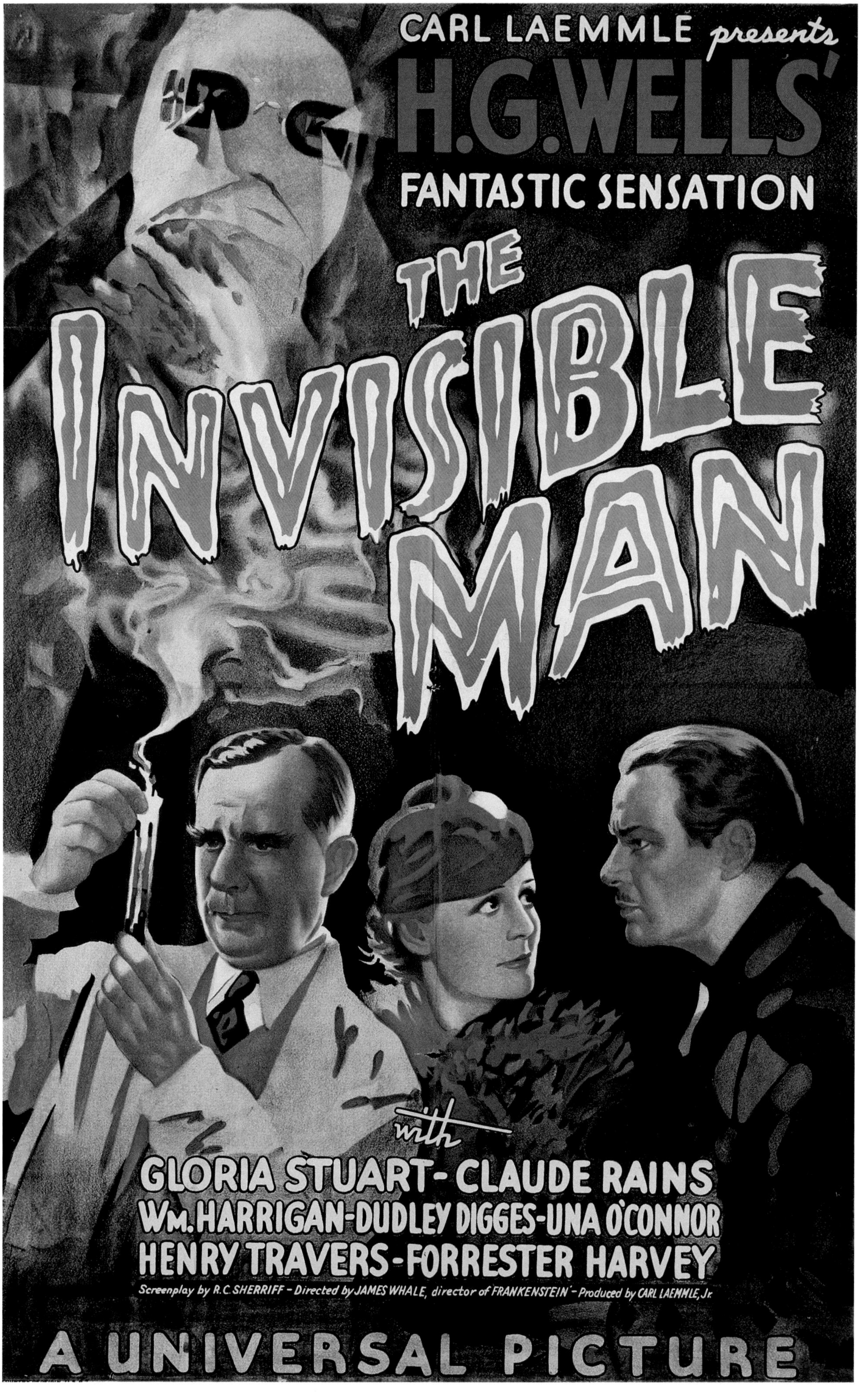

CARL LAEMMLE *presents*

H.G.WELLS'

FANTASTIC SENSATION

THE INVISIBLE MAN

*with*

GLORIA STUART · CLAUDE RAINS
WM. HARRIGAN · DUDLEY DIGGES · UNA O'CONNOR
HENRY TRAVERS · FORRESTER HARVEY

Screenplay by R.C. SHERRIFF · Directed by JAMES WHALE, *director of* FRANKENSTEIN · Produced by CARL LAEMMLE, Jr.

A UNIVERSAL PICTURE

13

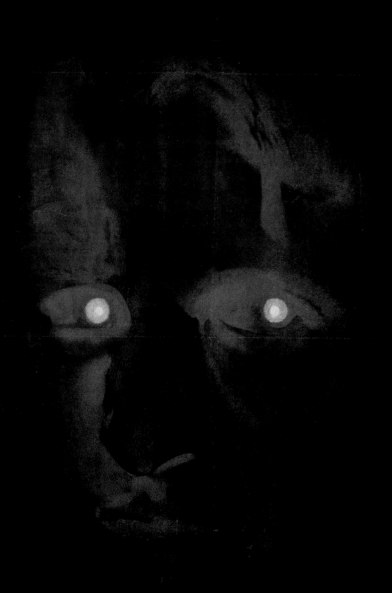

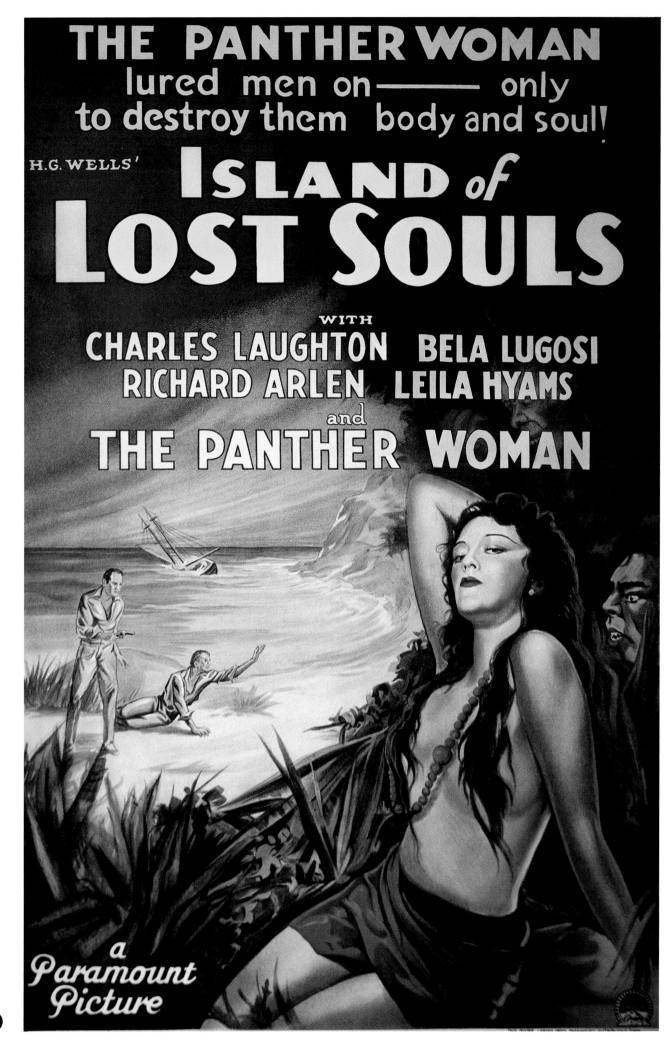

LOVE BATTLING AGAINST THE
SORCERY OF THE JUNGLE!

JACK HOLT *in*

"BLACK MOON"

*with* FAY WRAY DOROTHY BURGESS

From the Cosmopolitan Magazine novel by Clements Ripley
Directed by ROY WILLIAM NEILL

A COLUMBIA PICTURE

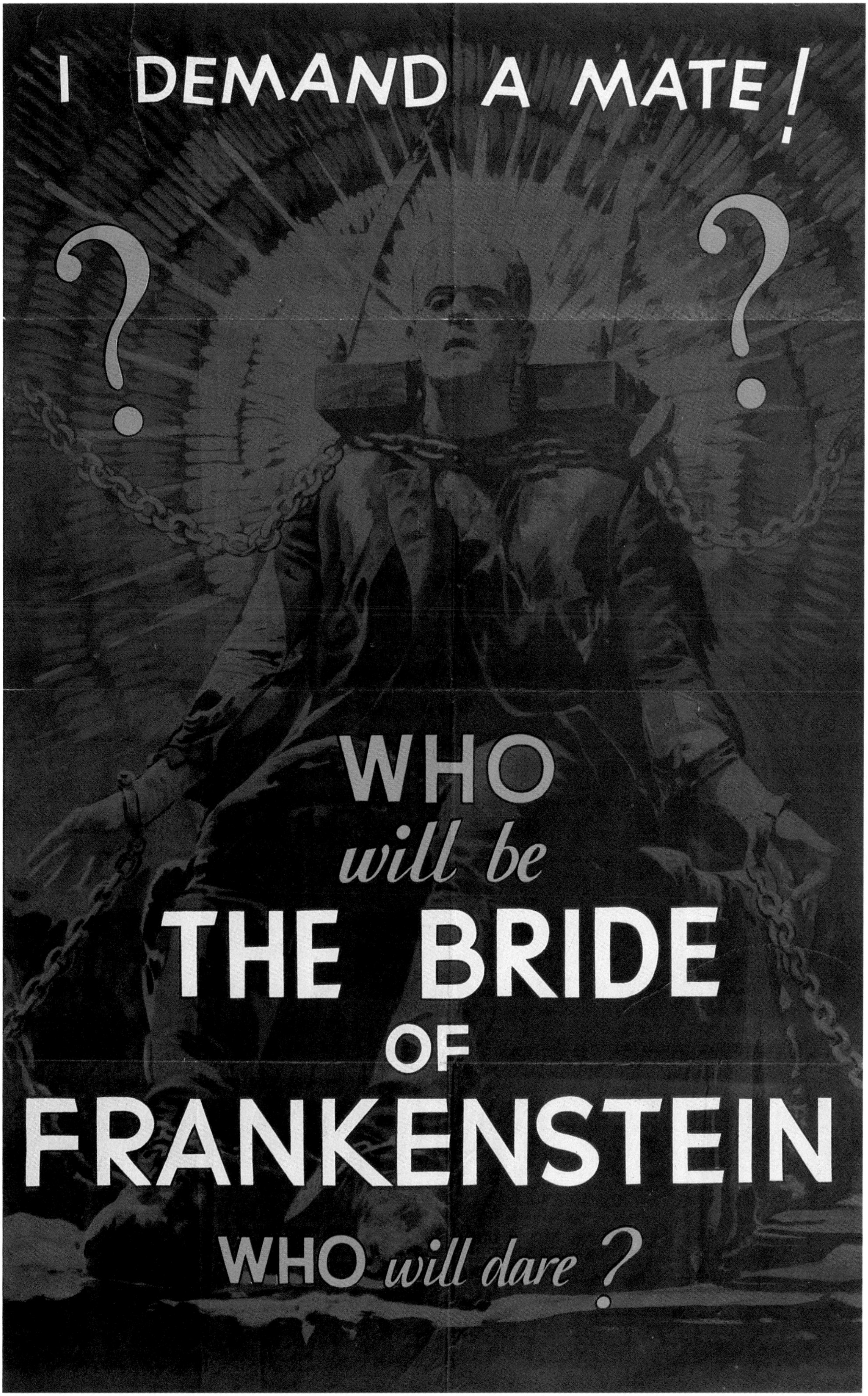
I DEMAND A MATE!
WHO
will be
THE BRIDE
OF
FRANKENSTEIN
WHO will dare?

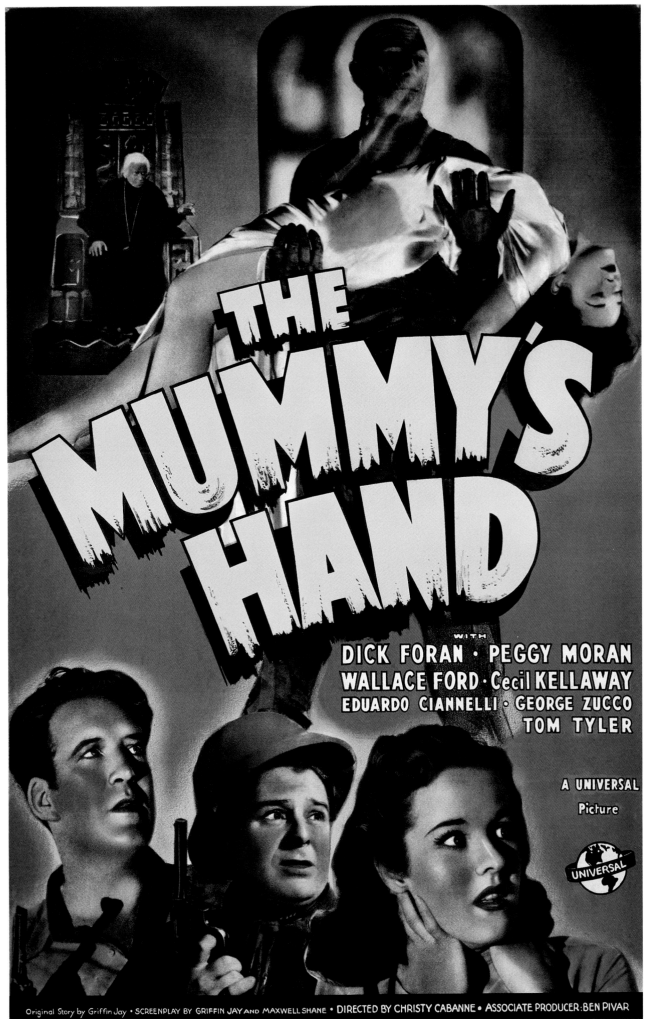

# THE MUMMY'S HAND

WITH

**DICK FORAN** • **PEGGY MORAN**
**WALLACE FORD** • Cecil **KELLAWAY**
**EDUARDO CIANNELLI** • **GEORGE ZUCCO**
**TOM TYLER**

A **UNIVERSAL**
Picture

Original Story by Griffin Jay • SCREENPLAY BY GRIFFIN JAY AND MAXWELL SHANE • DIRECTED BY CHRISTY CABANNE • ASSOCIATE PRODUCER: BEN PIVAR

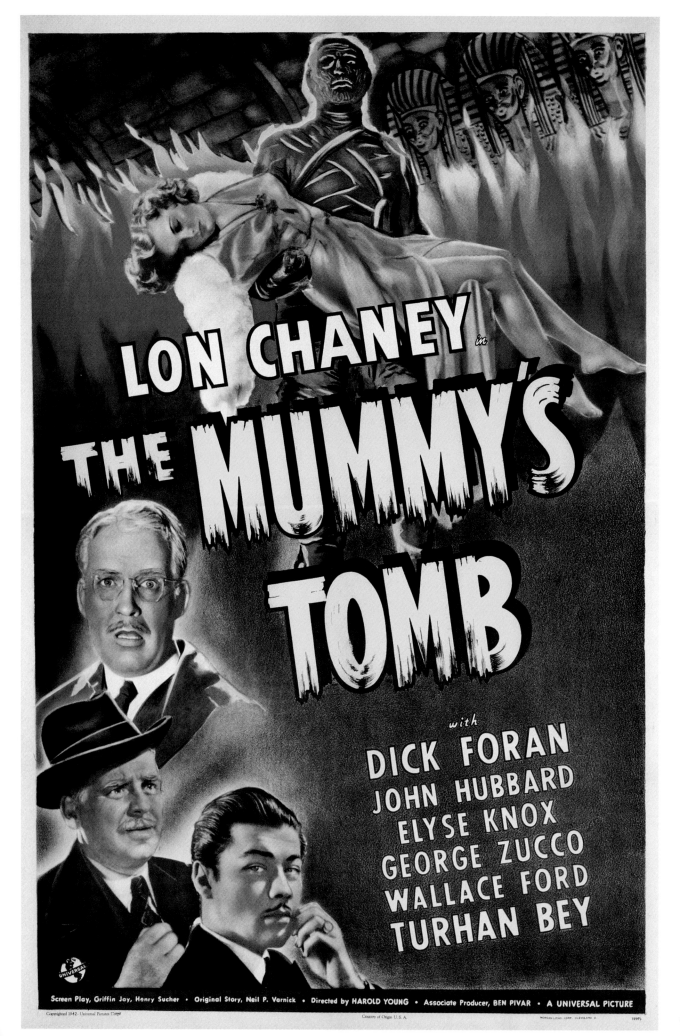

LON CHANEY *in*
THE MUMMY'S TOMB

*with*

DICK FORAN
JOHN HUBBARD
ELYSE KNOX
GEORGE ZUCCO
WALLACE FORD
TURHAN BEY

Screen Play, Griffin Jay, Henry Sucher · Original Story, Neil P. Varnick · Directed by HAROLD YOUNG · Associate Producer, BEN PIVAR · A UNIVERSAL PICTURE

THE CURSE OF THE Cat People

with

SIMONE SIMON
KENT SMITH
JANE RANDOLPH

PRODUCED BY VAL LEWTON
DIRECTED BY
GUNTHER V. FRITSCH and ROBERT WISE
SCREEN PLAY BY DeWITT BODEEN

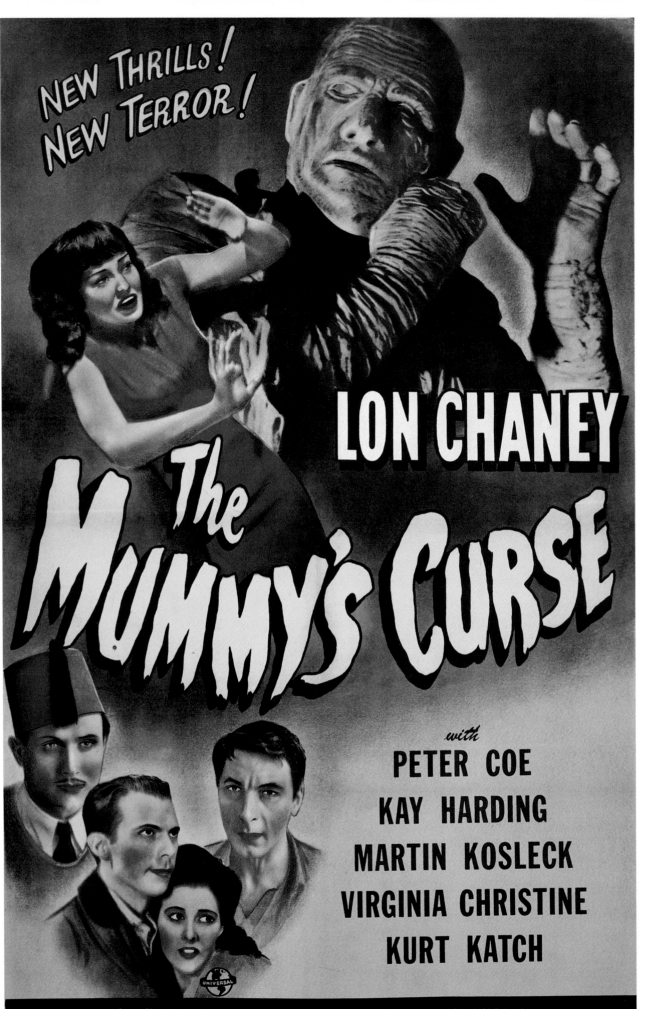

NEW THRILLS!
NEW TERROR!

LON CHANEY

The Mummy's Curse

with
PETER COE
KAY HARDING
MARTIN KOSLECK
VIRGINIA CHRISTINE
KURT KATCH

Screen Play by Bernard Schubert    Original Story and Adaptation by Leon Abrams and Dwight V. Babcock
Directed by LESLIE GOODWINS    Associate Producer, OLIVER DRAKE    A UNIVERSAL PICTURE

NO CHAINS CAN HOLD IT! NO TOMB CAN SEAL IT!

ALL NEW TERROR!

The MUMMY'S GHOST

Starring

LON CHANEY

as KHARIS, THE MUMMY

with

JOHN CARRADINE
RAMSAY AMES
BARTON MacLANE
GEORGE ZUCCO
ROBERT LOWERY

UNIVERSAL

Screen Play, Griffin Jay, Henry Sucher, Brenda Weisberg   Original Story, Griffin Jay and Henry Sucher   Directed by REGINALD LeBORG   Associate Producer, BEN PIVAR   A UNIVERSAL PICTURE

Copyrighted 1944 Universal Pictures Corp.          Country of Origin U.S.A.                    MORGAN LITHO. CORP. CLEVELAND, O.   26495

27

BORIS **KARLOFF** IN **ISLE OF THE DEAD**

WILL KEEP YOU SCREAMING!

with

**ELLEN DREW**

**MARC CRAMER**

Produced by
VAL LEWTON · Directed by
MARK ROBSON

WRITTEN BY ARDEL WRAY & JOSEF MISCHEL

RKO
RADIO
PICTURES

ALL NEW...
ALL TOGETHER!
FRANKENSTEIN'S
MONSTER
WOLF MAN
DRACULA
UNIVERSAL PRESENTS
HOUSE OF
DRACULA
MAD DOCTOR
HUNCHBACK
with
LON CHANEY MARTHA O'DRISCOLL
JOHN CARRADINE LIONEL ATWILL
ONSLOW STEVENS · GLENN STRANGE
JANE ADAMS · LUDWIG STOSSEL
UNIVERSAL
Original Screenplay by Edward T. Lowe Directed by ERLE C. KENTON Produced by PAUL MALVERN Executive Producer JOE GERSHENSON 45/376
Copyrighted 1945 Universal Pictures Corp. Country of Origin U.S.A.

Boris KARLOFF

in

ROBERT LOUIS STEVENSON'S
THE Body Snatcher

with BELA LUGOSI

HENRY DANIELL
EDITH ATWATER
RUSSELL WADE
SHARYN MOFFETT

RKO RADIO PICTURES

PRODUCED BY VAL LEWTON · DIRECTED BY ROBERT WISE
WRITTEN FOR THE SCREEN BY PHILIP MacDONALD
AND CARLOS KEITH

"A Thriller...THE CRITICS HUGGED IT!"
Walter Winchell

J. ARTHUR RANK
presents

DEAD OF NIGHT

A UNIVERSAL RELEASE WITH

MERVYN JOHNS
ROLAND CULVER
FREDERICK VALK
SALLY ANN HOWES
GOOGIE WITHERS
MICHAEL REDGRAVE

Screenplay by John Baines and Angus Macphail • Based on Original Stories by E.F. Benson and John Baines
Directed by CAVALCANTI, BASIL DEARDEN, ROBERT HAMER • Associate Producers: SIDNEY COLE and JOHN CROYDON • Produced by MICHAEL BALCON    46/971

31

MOON MONSTERS LAUNCH ATTACK AGAINST EARTH!
HOW CAN SCIENCE MEET THE MENACE of ASTRAL ASSASSINS? New SCIENCE-FICTION THRILLS!
3D
ADVENTURES INTO THE FUTURE in New TRU-3 DIMENSION!
ROBOT MONSTER
RELEASED THRU ASTOR PICTURES CORP.
with GEORGE NADER
CLAUDIA BARRETT
Produced by AL ZIMBALIST
PRINTED IN U. S. A.

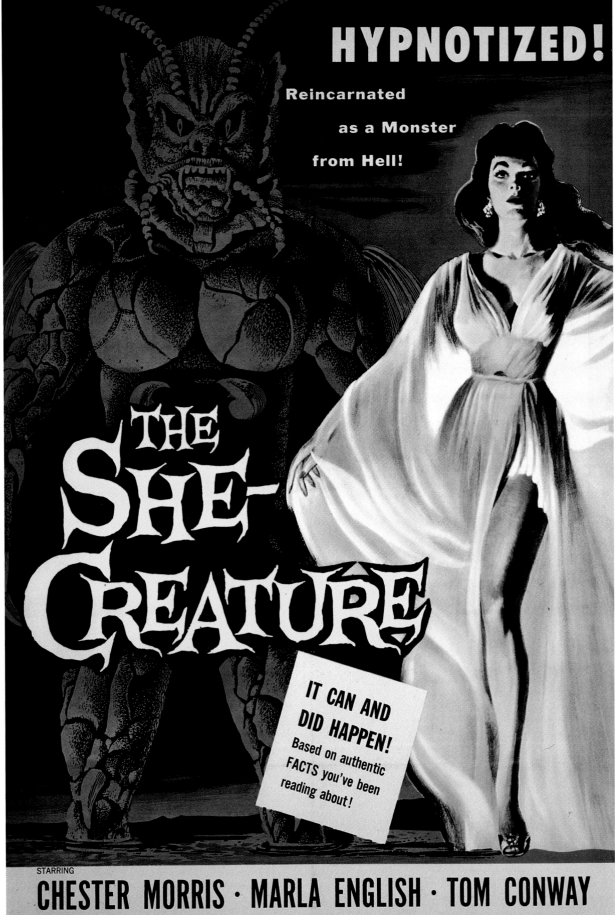

HYPNOTIZED!

Reincarnated
as a Monster
from Hell!

# THE SHE-CREATURE

**IT CAN AND DID HAPPEN!** Based on authentic FACTS you've been reading about!

STARRING

## CHESTER MORRIS · MARLA ENGLISH · TOM CONWAY

CATHY DOWNS · LANCE FULLER · RON RANDELL · Freida Inescort A GOLDEN STATE Production

Produced by ALEX GORDON · Executive Producer SAMUEL Z. ARKOFF · Directed by EDWARD L. CAHN · Screenplay by LOU RUSOFF · Based on an original idea by JERRY ZIGMOND

Associate Producer ISRAEL M. BERMAN · Distributed by AMERICAN INTERNATIONAL PICTURES

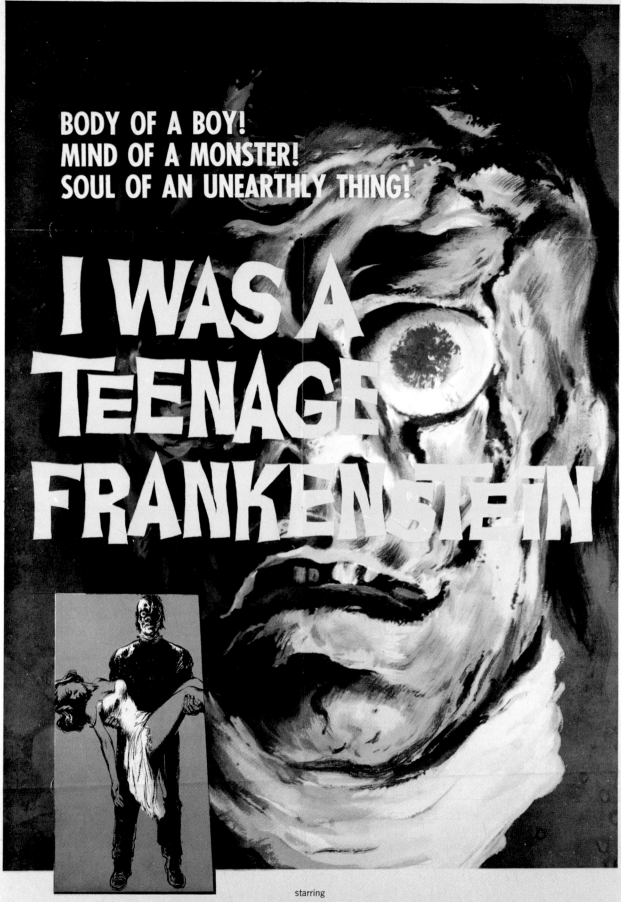

BODY OF A BOY!
MIND OF A MONSTER!
SOUL OF AN UNEARTHLY THING!

# I WAS A TEENAGE FRANKENSTEIN

starring

WHIT **BISSELL** · PHYLLIS **COATES** · ROBERT **BURTON** · GARY **CONWAY**

Produced by **HERMAN COHEN** · Directed by **HERBERT L. STROCK** · Screenplay by **KENNETH LANGTRY**

A JAMES H. NICHOLSON-SAMUEL Z. ARKOFF PRODUCTION · AN AMERICAN INTERNATIONAL PICTURE

The most amazing
motion picture
of our time!

# I WAS A TEENAGE WEREWOLF

starring

MICHAEL LANDON · YVONNE LIME · WHIT BISSELL · TONY MARSHALL

Produced by HERMAN COHEN · Directed by GENE FOWLER Jr. · Screenplay by RALPH THORNTON

A JAMES NICHOLSON-SAMUEL ARKOFF Production · AN AMERICAN INTERNATIONAL PICTURE

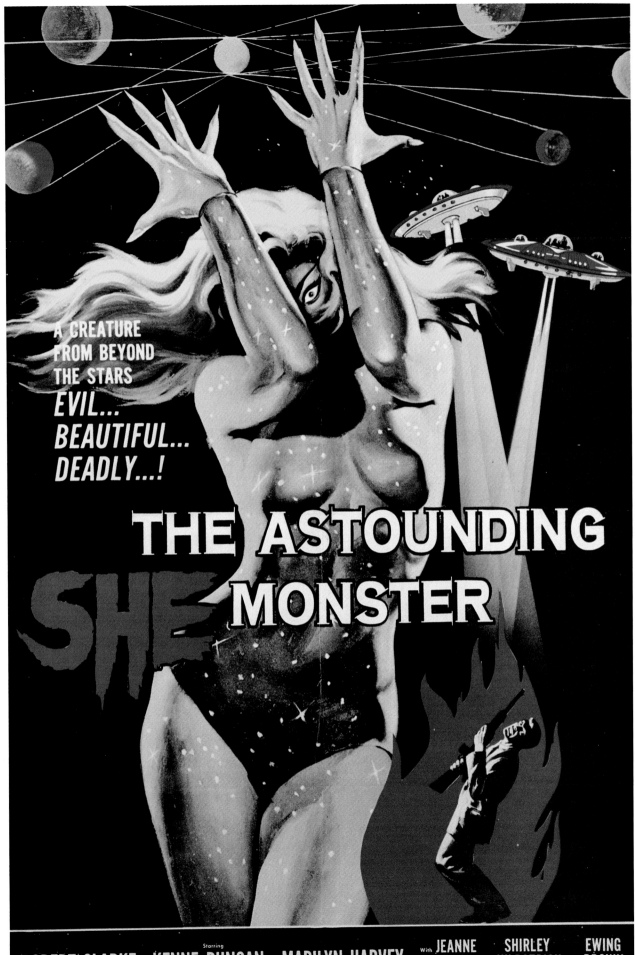

A CREATURE
FROM BEYOND
THE STARS
*EVIL...*
*BEAUTIFUL...*
*DEADLY...!*

THE ASTOUNDING
SHE MONSTER

Starring
ROBERT CLARKE · KENNE DUNCAN · MARILYN HARVEY · With JEANNE TATUM · SHIRLEY KILPATRICK · EWING BROWN
Story and Screenplay by FRANK HALL · Produced and Directed by RONNIE ASHCROFT · A HOLLYWOOD INTERNATIONAL Production
An AMERICAN INTERNATIONAL Release

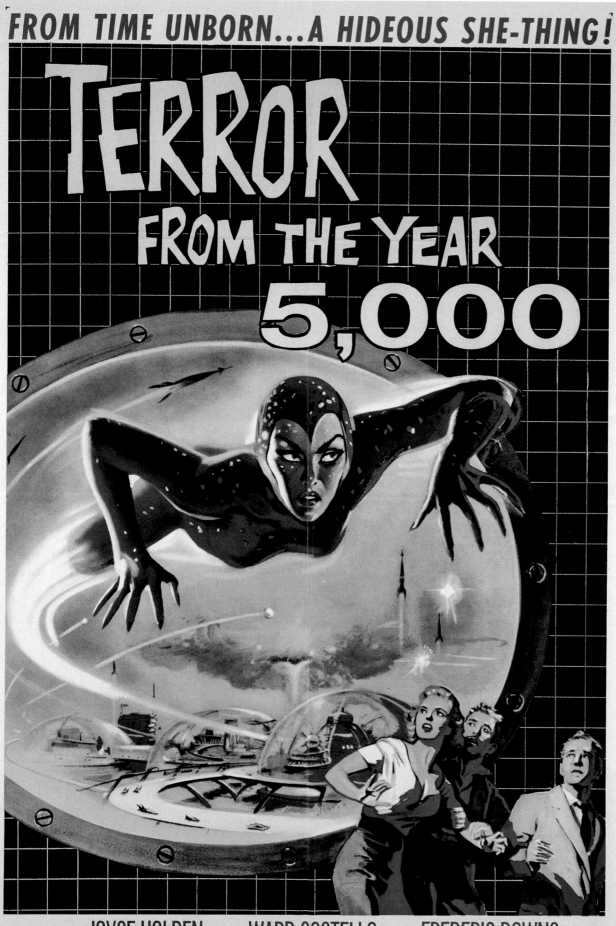

FROM TIME UNBORN...A HIDEOUS SHE-THING!

# TERROR FROM THE YEAR 5,000

starring JOYCE HOLDEN · WARD COSTELLO · FREDERIC DOWNS

Produced, Directed and Written by ROBERT J. GURNEY · A JAMES H. NICHOLSON and SAMUEL Z. ARKOFF PRODUCTION · AN AMERICAN-INTERNATIONAL PICTURE

40

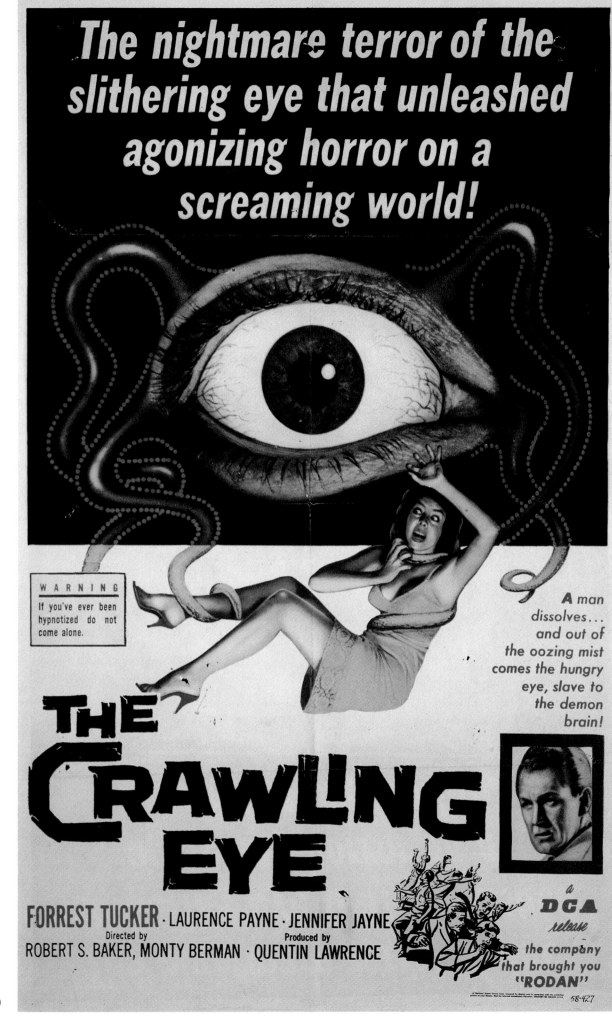

The nightmare terror of the slithering eye that unleashed agonizing horror on a screaming world!

WARNING
If you've ever been hypnotized do not come alone.

A man dissolves... and out of the oozing mist comes the hungry eye, slave to the demon brain!

THE CRAWLING EYE

FORREST TUCKER · LAURENCE PAYNE · JENNIFER JAYNE
Directed by
ROBERT S. BAKER, MONTY BERMAN · Produced by QUENTIN LAWRENCE

a DCA release
the company that brought you "RODAN"

58-427

41

# HOUSE ON HAUNTED HILL

starring **VINCENT PRICE**

CAROL OHMART · RICHARD LONG

ALAN MARSHAL · AN ALLIED ARTISTS PICTURE

Produced and Directed by **WILLIAM CASTLE** · Written by **ROBB WHITE**

# The CURSE OF THE WEREWOLF

in Eastman **COLOR**

FLESH CRAWLS!
BLOOD CURDLES!
PHIBES LIVES!

DR. PHIBES RISES AGAIN!

JAMES H. NICHOLSON and SAMUEL Z. ARKOFF Present

VINCENT PRICE   ROBERT QUARRY

Guest Stars: PETER CUSHING   BERYL REID   TERRY-THOMAS

Written By ROBERT FUEST and ROBERT BLEES   Based on Characters Created By JAMES WHITON and WILLIAM GOLDSTEIN

Directed By ROBERT FUEST   Executive Producers: SAMUEL Z. ARKOFF and JAMES H. NICHOLSON   Produced By LOUIS M. HEYWARD

Original Music Composed By JOHN GALE   An AMERICAN INTERNATIONAL Picture   Color Prints By DE LUXE®

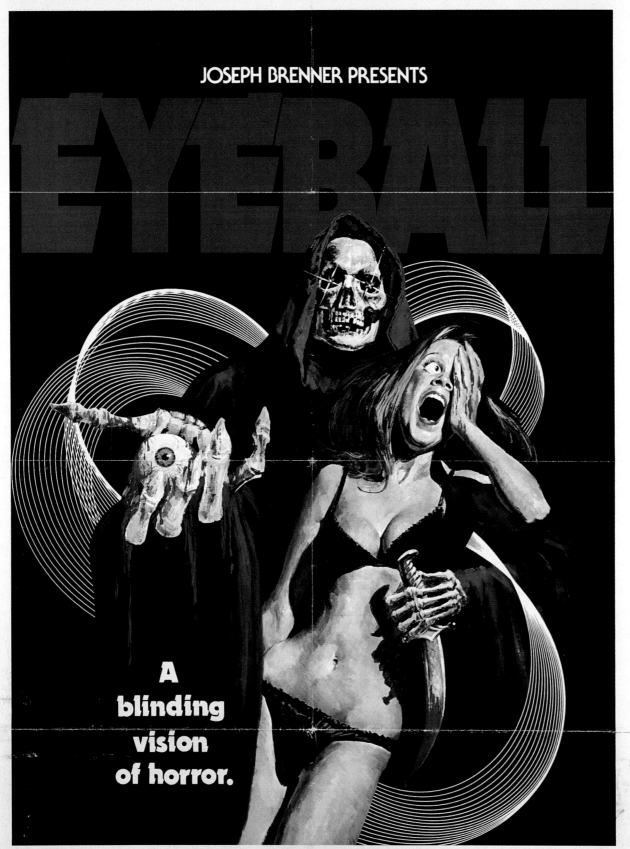

# A STABBING NIGHTMARE BECOMES A LIVING TERROR!

JOSEPH BRENNER PRESENTS

# EYEBALL

A blinding vision of horror.

JOSEPH BRENNER PRESENTS
"EYEBALL"

Starring
JOHN RICHARDSON · MARTINE BROCHARD · INES PELLEGRIN · SILVIA SOLAR · GEORGE RIGAUD
Directed by UMBERTO LENZI · Executive Producer JOSEPH BRENNER
A JOSEPH BRENNER ASSOCIATES, INC. RELEASE · IN COLOR

**R** RESTRICTED
UNDER 17 REQUIRES ACCOMPANYING
PARENT OR ADULT GUARDIAN

46

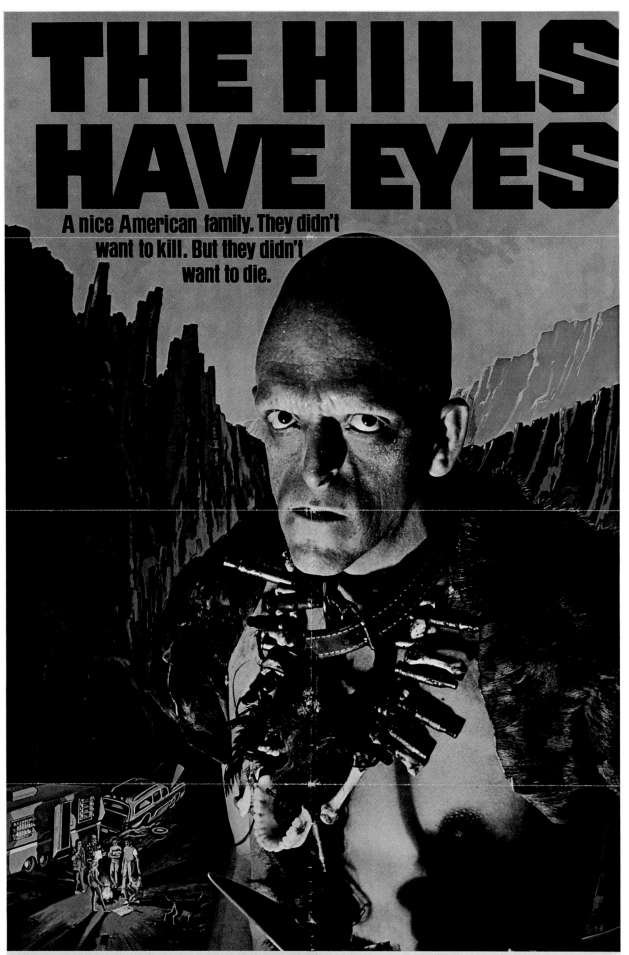

# THE HILLS HAVE EYES

A nice American family. They didn't
want to kill. But they didn't
want to die.

PETER LOCKE PRESENTS A FILM BY WES CRAVEN **THE HILLS HAVE EYES** STARRING SUSAN LANIER, ROBERT HOUSTON, MARTIN SPEER
ALSO STARRING DEE WALLACE, RUSS GRIEVE, JOHN STEADMAN, MICHAEL BERRYMAN & VIRGINIA VINCENT AS ETHEL CARTER                    COLOR BY MGM

JAMES WHITWORTH AS JUPITER     DIRECTOR OF PHOTOGRAPHY ERIC SAARINEN MUSIC BY DON PEAKE                          R RESTRICTED

WRITTEN & DIRECTED BY WES CRAVEN (WRITER & DIRECTOR OF LAST HOUSE ON THE LEFT)     PRODUCED BY PETER LOCKE      A VANGUARD RELEASE

# HALLOWEEN

The
Night
*He*
Came
Home!

MOUSTAPHA AKKAD PRESENTS DONALD PLEASENCE IN JOHN CARPENTER'S "HALLOWEEN"
WITH JAMIE LEE CURTIS, P.J. SOLES, NANCY LOOMIS · WRITTEN BY JOHN CARPENTER AND DEBRA HILL
EXECUTIVE PRODUCER IRWIN YABLANS · DIRECTED BY JOHN CARPENTER · PRODUCED BY DEBRA HILL
PANAVISION® TECHNICOLOR® A COMPASS INTERNATIONAL RELEASE Φ R RESTRICTED

49

Just when you thought
it was safe
to go back in the water...

# JAWS 2

Coming to theatres everywhere June 16th.

# MOTEL HELL

## It takes all kinds of critters to make Farmer Vincent Fritters

You might just die... laughing!

"MOTEL HELL" starring RORY CALHOUN   PAUL LINKE   NANCY PARSONS   NINA AXELROD and WOLFMAN JACK   produced by STEVEN-CHARLES JAFFE and ROBERT JAFFE executive producer HERB JAFFE   written by ROBERT JAFFE and STEVEN-CHARLES JAFFE directed by KEVIN CONNOR   music by LANCE RUBIN   ☰ United Artists
A Transamerica Company

ENTER THE SECRET GARDEN IN ᴅᴏ DOLBY STEREO ™
IN SELECTED THEATRES

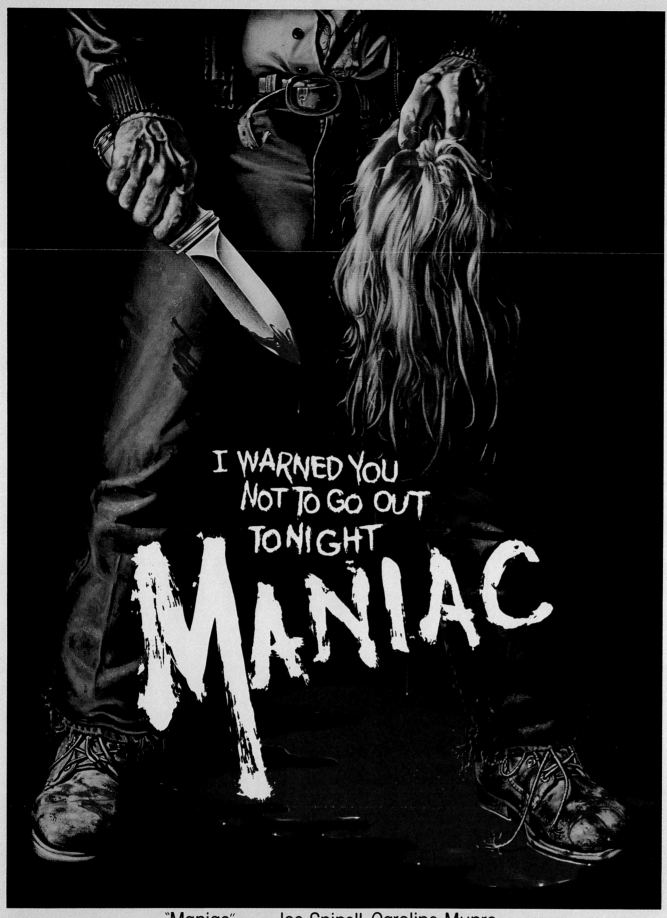

I WARNED YOU
NOT TO GO OUT
TO NIGHT

# MANIAC

"Maniac" Starring Joe Spinell · Caroline Munro

Associate Producer John Packard · Special Make-Up Effects by Tom Savini · Music by Jay Chattaway · Screenplay by C.A. Rosenberg and Joe Spinell · Executive Producers Joe Spinell and Judd Hamilton

Produced by Andrew Garroni and William Lustig · Directed by William Lustig

A Magnum Motion Picture · Copyright ©1980 Maniac Productions
Color by TVC

RECORDED IN
DOLBY STEREO

Distributed by ANALYSIS FILM CORPORATION
A NEW FILM DISTRIBUTION COMPANY

There is no explicit sex in this picture.
However, there are scenes of violence which may be considered horrifying.
No one under 17 will be admitted.

"...The most ferociously original horror film of the year..."
—Stephen King
author of *Carrie* and *The Shining*

# THE EVIL DEAD

Starring BRUCE CAMPBELL ELLEN SANDWEISS HAL DELRICH BETSY BAKER SARAH YORK
Make-up Effects by TOM SULLIVAN Photographic Effects by BART PIERCE Photography by TIM PHILO
Music by JOE LoDUCA Produced by ROBERT G. TAPERT Written and Directed by SAM RAIMI
Color by TECHNICOLOR® Renaissance Pictures Ltd. From NEW LINE CINEMA All Rights Reserved

53

# THE TENANT IN ROOM 7 IS VERY SMALL, VERY TWISTED, AND VERY MAD

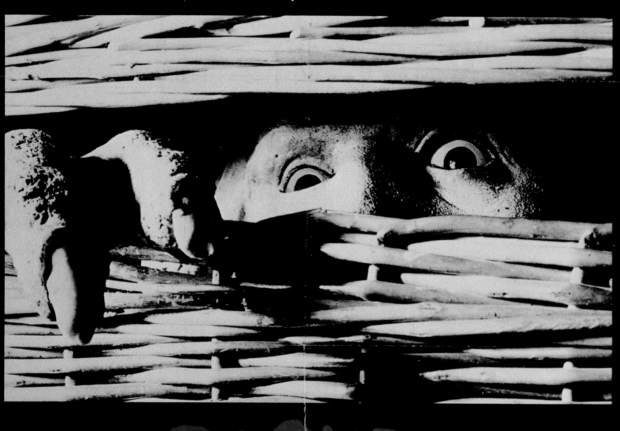

**BASKET CASE**

an IEVINS / HENENLOTTER production    starring KEVIN VanHENTENRYCK  TERRI SUSAN SMITH
BEVERLY BONNER   Director of Photography BRUCE TORBET   Music GUS RUSSO
Executive Producers ARNIE BRUCK   TOM KAYE   Production Executive RAY SUNDLIN
Produced by EDGAR IEVINS   Written and Directed by FRANK HENENLOTTER

 **DISTRIBUTED BY**
# RUGGED FILMS INC.

IF NANCY DOESN'T WAKE UP SCREAMING
SHE WON'T WAKE UP AT ALL.

WES CRAVEN'S *A Nightmare*
ON ELM STREET

NEW LINE CINEMA, MEDIA HOME ENTERTAINMENT, INC. and SMART EGG PICTURES Present
A ROBERT SHAYE Production • A WES CRAVEN Film • "A NIGHTMARE ON ELM STREET"
Starring JOHN SAXON • RONEE BLAKLEY • HEATHER LANGENKAMP • AMANDA WYSS • NICK CORRI • JOHNNY DEPP and ROBERT ENGLUND as Fred Krueger
Music by CHARLES BERNSTEIN • Director of Photography JACQUES HAITKIN • Editor RICK SHAINE • Executive Producers STANLEY DUDELSON and JOSEPH WOLF
Co-Producer SARA RISHER • Produced by ROBERT SHAYE • Written and Directed by WES CRAVEN  FROM NEW LINE CINEMA

R RESTRICTED
UNDER 17 REQUIRES ACCOMPANYING
PARENT OR ADULT GUARDIAN

© New Line Cinema Corp. MCMLXXXIV

57

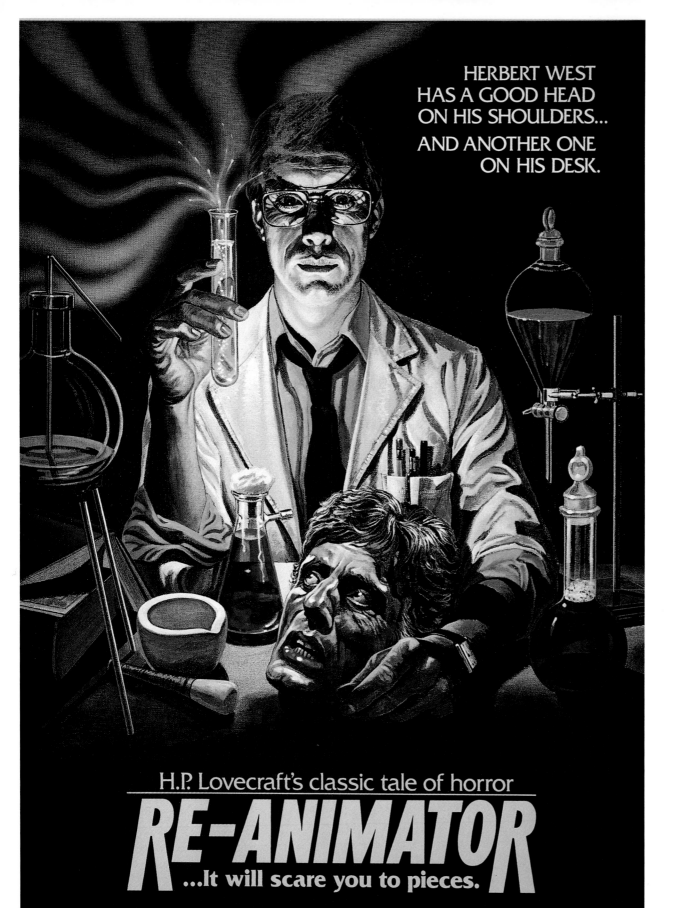

HERBERT WEST
HAS A GOOD HEAD
ON HIS SHOULDERS...
AND ANOTHER ONE
ON HIS DESK.

H.P. Lovecraft's classic tale of horror

# RE-ANIMATOR

...It will scare you to pieces.

BRIAN YUZNA PRESENTS "H.P. LOVECRAFT'S RE-ANIMATOR" STARRING BRUCE ABBOTT  BARBARA CRAMPTON  DAVID GALE  ROBERT SAMPSON AND JEFFREY COMBS AS HERBERT WEST
EXECUTIVE PRODUCERS MICHAEL AVERY AND BRUCE CURTIS  ASSOCIATE PRODUCERS BOB GREENBERG AND CHARLES DONALD STOREY  DIRECTOR OF PHOTOGRAPHY MAC AHLBERG  MUSIC COMPOSED BY RICHARD BAND
SCREENPLAY BY DENNIS PAOLI  WILLIAM J. NORRIS AND STUART GORDON  BASED ON H.P. LOVECRAFT'S "HERBERT WEST — THE RE-ANIMATOR"  SPECIAL EFFECTS MAKE-UP ANTHONY DOUBLIN AND JOHN NAULIN
ADDITIONAL MAKE-UP EFFECTS JOHN BUECHLER  PRODUCED BY BRIAN YUZNA  DIRECTED BY STUART GORDON

WARNING! This motion picture contains scenes of horror that may be considered too intense for anyone under the age of 18.

AN EMPIRE PICTURES RELEASE

# CREEPOZOIDS

YOUR FLESH WILL CRAWL RIGHT OFF YOUR BONES.

TITAN PRODUCTIONS Presents "CREEPOZOIDS" Starring LINNEA QUIGLEY, KEN ABRAHAM, MICHAEL ARANDA, RICHARD HAWKINS, KIM McKAMY and JOI WILSON Music Composed by GUY MOON Production Designer ROYCE MATHEW Special Make-up and Creature Effects by NEXT GENERATION EFFECTS, INC. THOM FLOUTZ and PETER CARSILLO Special Mechanical Effects by JOHN CRISWELL Director of Photography THOMAS CALLAWAY Edited by MIRIAM L. PREISSEL Written by BURFORD HAUSER and DAVID DeCOTEAU Produced by DAVID DeCOTEAU and JOHN SCHOUWEILER Directed by DAVID DeCOTEAU

Urban Classics

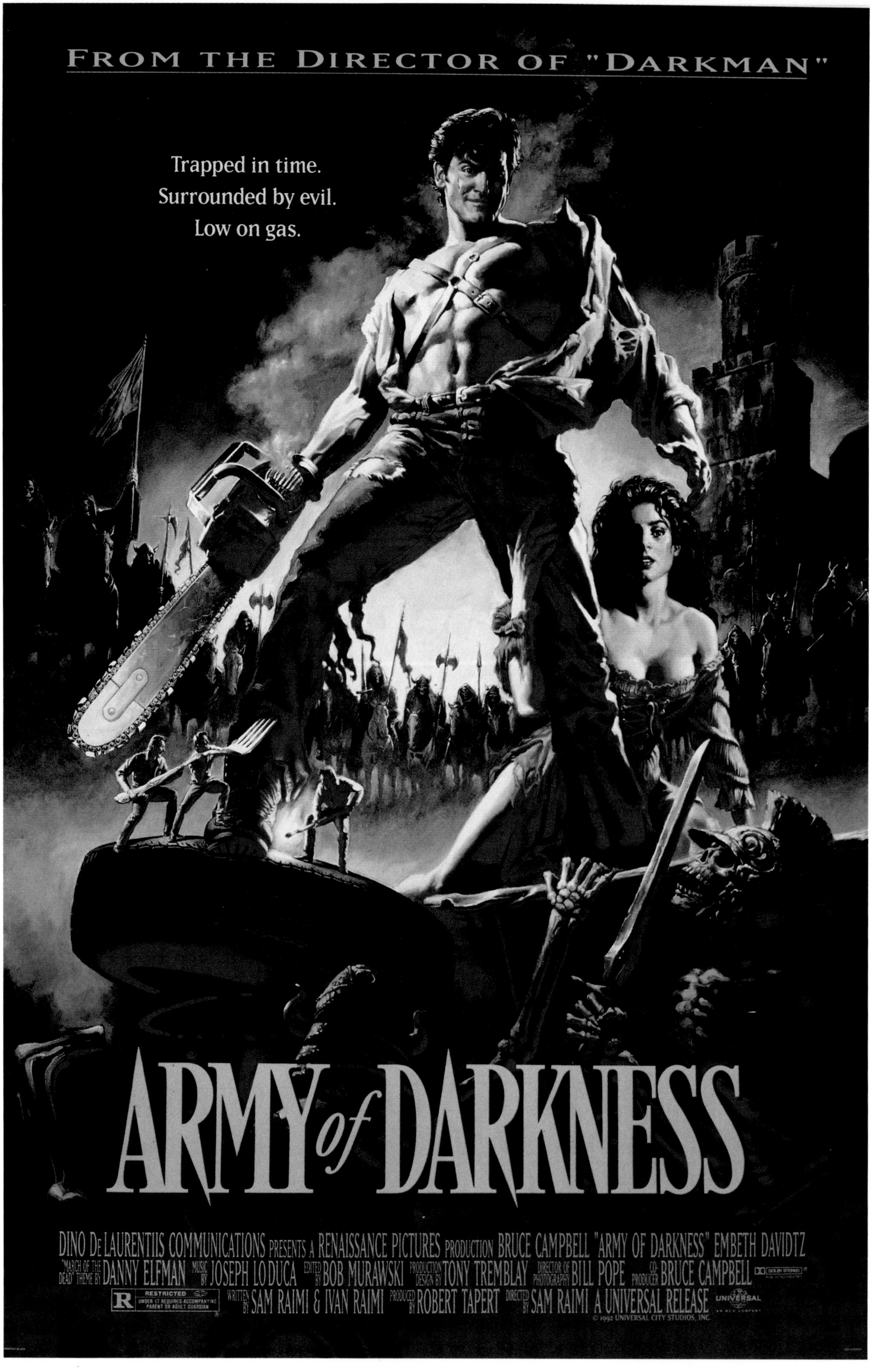
FROM THE DIRECTOR OF "DARKMAN"
Trapped in time.
Surrounded by evil.
Low on gas.
ARMY of DARKNESS
DINO DE LAURENTIIS COMMUNICATIONS PRESENTS A RENAISSANCE PICTURES PRODUCTION BRUCE CAMPBELL "ARMY OF DARKNESS" EMBETH DAVIDTZ
"MARCH OF THE DEAD" THEME BY DANNY ELFMAN MUSIC BY JOSEPH LO DUCA EDITED BY BOB MURAWSKI PRODUCTION DESIGN BY TONY TREMBLAY DIRECTOR OF PHOTOGRAPHY BILL POPE CO-PRODUCER BRUCE CAMPBELL
R RESTRICTED UNDER 17 REQUIRES ACCOMPANYING PARENT OR ADULT GUARDIAN
WRITTEN BY SAM RAIMI & IVAN RAIMI PRODUCED BY ROBERT TAPERT DIRECTED BY SAM RAIMI A UNIVERSAL RELEASE
UNIVERSAL
© 1992 UNIVERSAL CITY STUDIOS, INC.